Find it!

At the beach

Published by Richardson Publishing Group Limited.
www.richardsonpublishinggroup.com

10 9 8 7 6 5 4 3 2 1

© Richardson Publishing Group Ltd 2022.

Design by Junior London Ltd, junior.london. Illustration by Jonathan Mortimer.

ISBN is 978-1-913602-24-6

Printed and bound by Bell & Bain Ltd, 303 Burnfield Road, Thornliebank, Glasgow G46 7UQ.

The contents of this publication are believed correct at the time of printing. Nevertheless the publisher can accept no responsibility for errors, omissions, or changes in the detail given, or for any expense or loss thereby caused.

A catalogue record for this book is available from the British Library.

If you would like to comment on any aspect of this book, please contact us at:

E-mail: puzzles@richardsonpublishinggroup.com

🐦 Follow us on Twitter @puzzlesandgames
📷 instagram.com/richardsonpuzzlesandgames
f facebook.com/richardsonpuzzlesandgames

Contents

Introduction

Find it! books are designed to foster a love of learning and exploring the world through having fun.

Each of our books contain twenty-five things to find in the world around you, along with amazing facts and mind-bending puzzles.

Solutions to the puzzles can be found in the back of the book along with a place to make notes on your finds and a summary chart of the things to find. You can use the summary chart as an index to quickly locate your finds within the book or you can cut it out of the book and use it to find things on your travels!

Once you have found everything, there is a certificate at the very back of the book which you can ask a parent or guardian to complete and award to you!

For every 3 books completed, a parent or guardian can send us a message in order to receive a Find it! Super Spotter badge (T&Cs apply)! Simply fill in the form on our website at: richardsonpuzzlesandgames.com/superspotter

Happy finding!

Introduction

Tick this box when you have found the object. If you have a friend or sibling with you, why don't you set up a game to see who can find the most objects each?

Activity to complete!

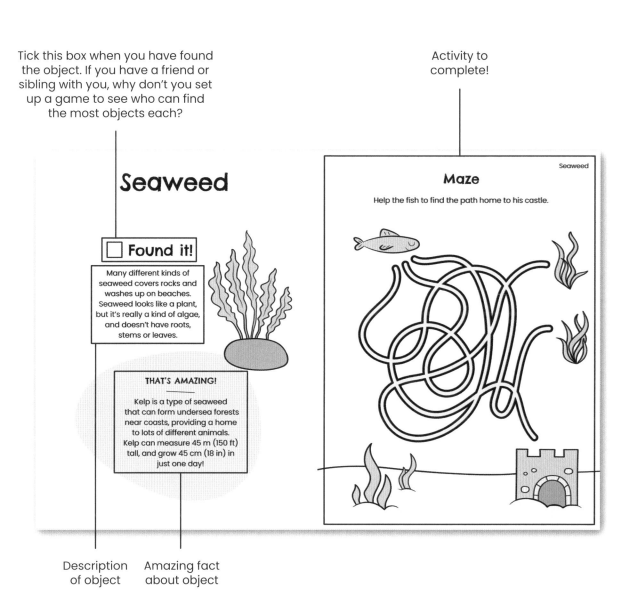

Seaweed

Found it!

Many different kinds of seaweed covers rocks and washes up on beaches. Seaweed looks like a plant, but it's really a kind of algae, and doesn't have roots, stems or leaves.

THAT'S AMAZING!

Kelp is a type of seaweed that can form undersea forests near coasts, providing a home to lots of different animals. Kelp can measure 45 m (150 ft) tall, and grow 45 cm (18 in) in just one day!

Seaweed

Maze

Help the fish to find the path home to his castle.

Description of object

Amazing fact about object

Seagull

☑ Found it!

Gulls are seabirds that swoop around coastlines and across the ocean, though sometimes they're found further inland. They eat fish, crabs and other small sea creatures – and sometimes they steal food from human seaside visitors!

THAT'S AMAZING!

There are more than 50 different types of gull. Most nest in big groups, which can number hundreds of thousands of gulls, and they often return to the same place to lay their eggs every year.

Complete the words

Complete the names of the seagull's snacks. The images next to the words are a clue. Cover them up if you would like to make the puzzle harder!

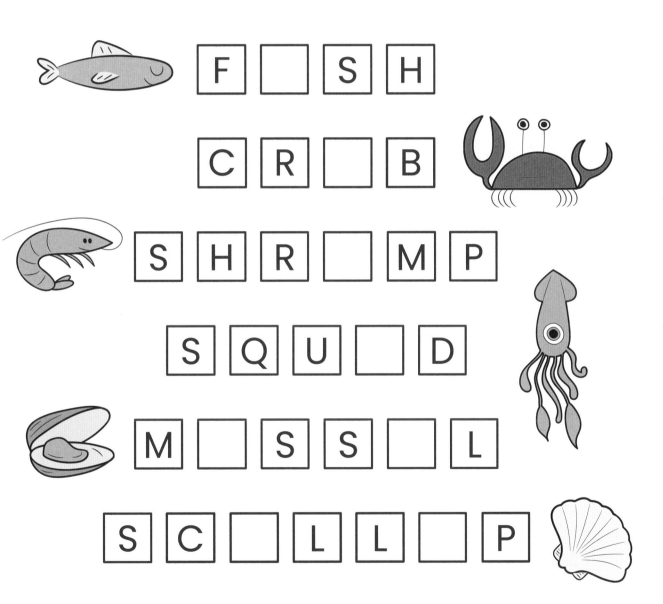

F [ ] S H

C R [ ] B

S H R [ ] M P

S Q U [ ] D

M [ ] S S [ ] L

S C [ ] L L [ ] P

Fish

 Found it!

Fish are animals that live in water and breathe through their gills. Some fish live in salty seawater, and some in freshwater.

THAT'S AMAZING!

There are many thousands of different kinds of fish. The biggest of all is the whale shark, which can grow to more than 12 m (40 ft) long.

Wordsearch

Look for the 10 words hidden in the wordsearch puzzle. The hidden words will run down and across. There are no words that run backwards or on a diagonal.

D	U	E	W	H	A	L	E	P	S
O	W	X	S	K	E	L	U	V	M
L	J	E	L	L	Y	F	I	S	H
P	L	O	B	S	T	E	R	Q	S
H	S	E	A	L	S	K	O	U	H
I	E	T	V	J	T	Y	J	I	A
N	C	R	A	B	L	L	L	D	R
U	O	C	T	O	P	U	S	E	K
S	H	S	T	I	N	G	R	A	Y
H	L	L	V	L	M	R	F	M	N

CRAB   OCTOPUS   SQUID

DOLPHIN   SEAL   STINGRAY

JELLYFISH   SHARK   WHALE

LOBSTER

Crab

☐ Found it!

Crabs have ten legs, with
claws for gripping on the front pair,
and a hard shell to protect them.
They can walk forwards, but they find
it quicker to scuttle sideways.

THAT'S AMAZING!

Unlike most crabs,
hermit crabs don't grow a
hard shell of their own.
They have to find shells to
protect them, and as they
grow bigger, they have to
swap to a bigger shell.

Dot to Dot

Connect the dots to uncover a picture,
then fill in with pens or pencils.

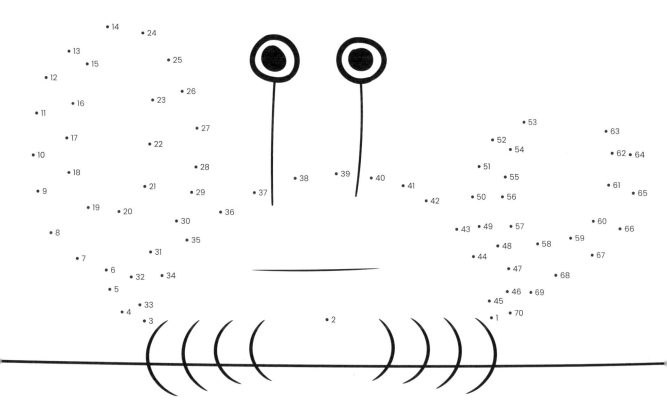

Shell

 **Found it!**

Seashells are homes for sea creatures. Every empty shell you find on a beach once contained an animal such as a snail, oyster, limpet or barnacle.

THAT'S AMAZING!

Some seashells are huge. Giant sea snails known as Australian trumpets or giant whelks have shells that can measure 70 cm (27.5 in) long!

Numbers

How many shells are there on the beach? If you find
10 more shells how many shells will there be in total?
Use the number line if you need it.

	+	10	=	
Beach				Total

0 1 2 3 4 5 6 7 8 9 10 11 12 13 14 15 16 17 18 19 20

Seaweed

☐ Found it!

Many different kinds of seaweed covers rocks and washes up on beaches. Seaweed looks like a plant, but it's really a kind of algae, and doesn't have roots, stems or leaves.

THAT'S AMAZING!

Kelp is a type of seaweed that can form undersea forests near coasts, providing a home to lots of different animals. Kelp can measure 45 m (150 ft) tall, and grow 45 cm (18 in) in just one day!

Maze

Help the fish to find the path home to his castle.

Rock pool

☐ Found it!

When the tide goes out on rocky coasts, pools of seawater are left behind. They are a bit warmer and saltier than the sea. If you look inside a rock pool you might spot little fish, seaweed, starfish, crabs and anemones.

THAT'S AMAZING!

Blennies are small fish that are often found in rock pools. Their eyes are on top of their heads so that they can keep a look out for gulls and other animals that might want to eat them.

Draw a picture

Draw a picture of something you find in the rock pool!

Sandcastle

☐ **Found it!**

Sandcastles are fun to make.
You could also build a sand car,
a sand mermaid, a sand dog
– or anything you like. Damp
sand is best for building.

THAT'S AMAZING!

The Magdalen Islands,
off the coast of Quebec,
Canada, holds a huge
sandcastle-building
competition every year.
It attracts hundreds of
sandcastle-builders and
thousands of visitors.

Complete the picture

Draw the other half of the sandcastle.

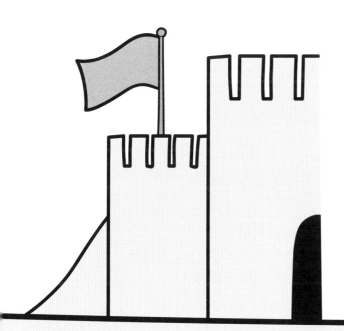

Sunshade

☑ **Found it!**

On a hot, sunny day, it's cooler underneath a sunshade, and you're less likely to burn your skin.

THAT'S AMAZING!

Temperatures are always measured using a thermometer shaded from direct sunlight. If you're sitting in the sunshine, it can feel much hotter.

Spot the difference

Can you spot 5 differences between the pictures?

Hat

☑ **Found it!**

Hats can keep us warm, and hats with a wide brim keep the Sun out of our eyes.

THAT'S AMAZING!

The world's most expensive hat is the Chapeau d'Amour ('Hat of Love' in French). Made of the precious metal platinum and covered in diamonds, it's valued at US $2.7 million.

Prices

What is the combined price of the 3 baseball caps?
Use the number line if you need it.

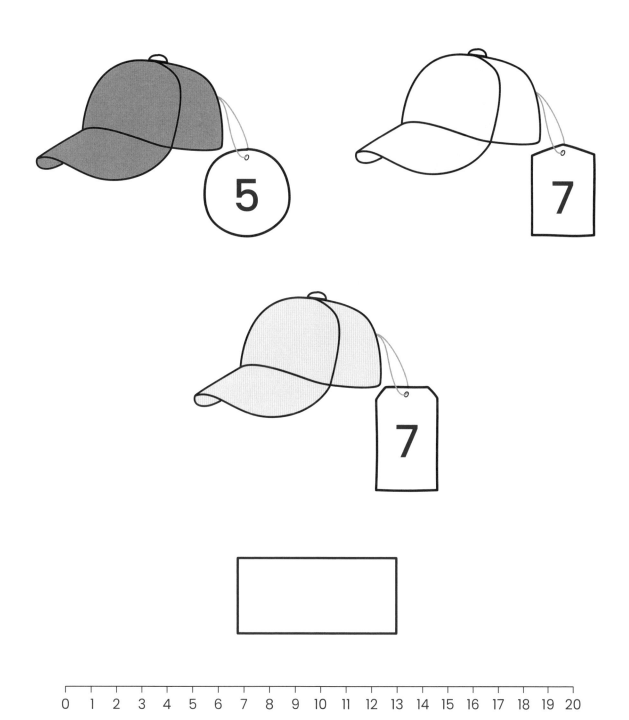

Sunscreen

☑ Found it!

The Sun can harm people's skin, even on a cloudy day, so it's important to apply sunscreen to skin that isn't covered up.

THAT'S AMAZING!

The 'SPF' you see on bottles of sunscreen stands for sun protection factor, and is a measure of the amount of protection the sunscreen gives your skin. The higher the number, the higher the protection.

Telling the time

The sunscreen will last for 1 hour. If the people put their sunscreen on at 1 o'clock, how long do they have before they will need to reapply?

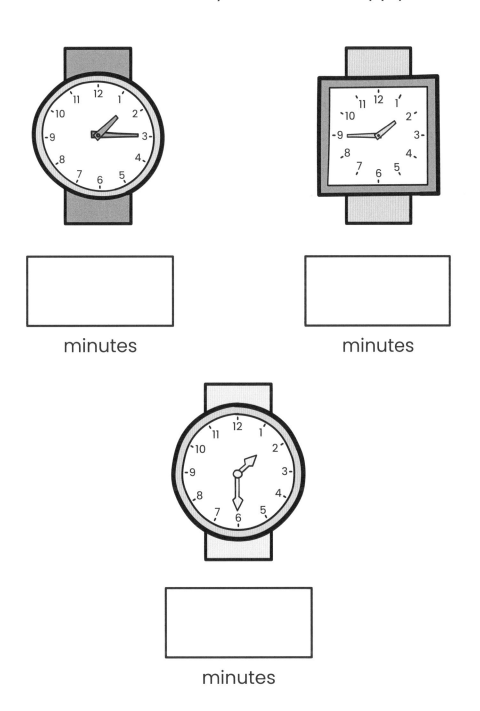

minutes

minutes

minutes

Towel

☐ Found it!

Towels are made of material that is good at soaking up water so that they dry you off quickly.

THAT'S AMAZING!

Towels are usually made from terrycloth, which is woven so that it includes tiny loops of thread. It's these little loops that make the towel good at absorbing water.

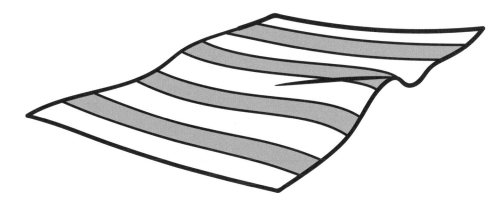

Numbers

Connect each person to a towel. How many people don't have a towel? Use the number line if you need it.

0 1 2 3 4 5 6 7 8 9 10 11 12 13 14 15 16 17 18 19 20

Ice cream

☑ **Found it!**

Ice cream is a
delicious frozen
treat on a hot day.

THAT'S AMAZING!

The first ice cream cones were
made in 1904 so that people could
enjoy ice cream at the same time
as walking around a big exhibition
called the World's Fair, which was
held in St. Louis, Missouri, USA.

Maze

Guide the ice cream truck to the beach.

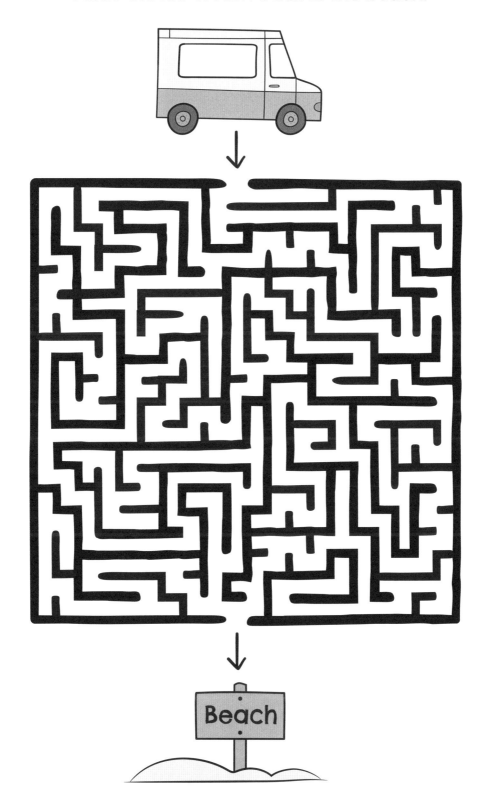

Drink

☑ Found it!

You need to drink plenty of water to stay healthy. A cold drink makes you feel cooler on a hot day.

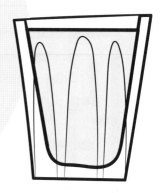

THAT'S AMAZING!

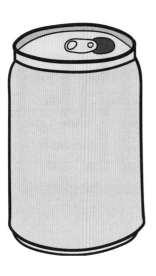

Fizzy drinks contain bubbles of the gas carbon dioxide. They were invented around 250 years ago by an English scientist called Joseph Priestley, who made the first ever sparkling water.

Fractions

Circle the bottles that are half full.

Ball

☐ Found it!

Balls are great fun to play with, and there are hundreds of different games you can play with them, including volleyball, tennis, baseball, netball, golf . . . and catch.

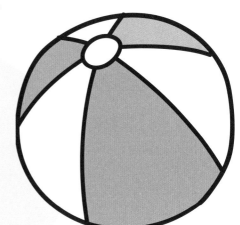

THAT'S AMAZING!

There are golf balls on the Moon – astronaut Alan Shepard had a game of Moon golf when he visited the Moon in 1971.

Wordsearch

Look for the 10 words hidden in the wordsearch puzzle. The hidden words will run down and across. There are no words that run backwards or on a diagonal.

R	W	C	R	O	Q	U	E	T	V
A	B	G	O	L	F	O	G	T	O
S	O	F	T	B	A	L	L	E	L
I	W	S	Q	U	A	S	H	N	L
T	L	N	S	V	R	K	T	N	E
K	I	A	P	O	L	O	A	I	Y
P	N	E	H	E	T	E	I	S	B
L	G	R	G	Z	O	F	K	T	A
A	P	O	O	L	W	R	Q	F	L
B	A	S	K	E	T	B	A	L	L

BASKETBALL   POLO   SQUASH
BOWLING   POOL   TENNIS
CROQUET   SOFTBALL   VOLLEYBALL
GOLF

Flying disk

☑ Found it!

To become really good at playing with a flying disc, you need to work on flicking your wrist as you throw.

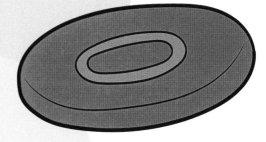

THAT'S AMAZING!

———

Ultimate is a team sport that uses a flying disk, with a playing field 110 m (360 ft) long by 37 m (121 ft) wide – about the same length as an American football field, but narrower.

Copy the patterns

Copy the patterns onto the flying disks.

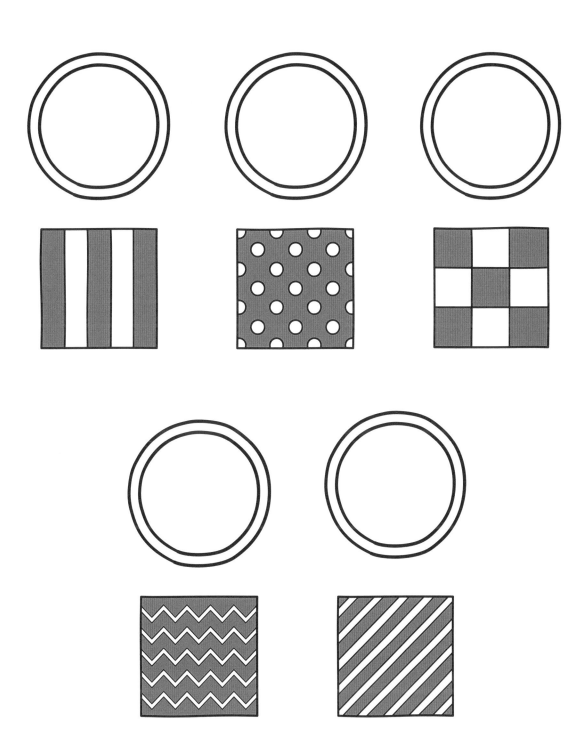

Bucket

☐ Found it!

Buckets are useful for carrying sand, water and other liquids. The ones used for making sandcastles are usually made of plastic.

THAT'S AMAZING!

A bucket used to be a unit of measurement a long time ago. One bucket was the same as about 18 l (4.8 US gallons).

Complete the words

Complete the names of things you can carry in a bucket. The images next to the words are a clue. Cover them up if you would like to make the puzzle harder!

M [ ] D

S [ ] N D

R [ ] C K S

S H [ ] L L S

W [ ] T [ ] R

F [ ] S S [ ] L S

Spade

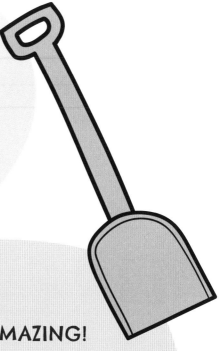

☑ Found it!

Spades are useful for
digging, especially
when you're making
a sandcastle.

THAT'S AMAZING!
———

The first spades, used
thousands of years ago,
were animal bones, often the
shoulder blades of big animals
such as oxen.

Matching pair

Circle the 2 spades that are the same.

Net

☐ **Found it!**

Nets are made from thin strands of material in a grid pattern, and are often used to catch fish. Fishing boats sail out to sea with huge nets, which can be miles long.

THAT'S AMAZING!

Pieces of a fishing net found in Antrea, Finland, are more than 10,000 years old! The net was made from willow, and had sunk to the bottom of a lake, along with fishing floats and weights to keep the net ready for its catch.

Dot to dot

Connect the dots to find out what's in the
net, then fill in with pens or pencils.

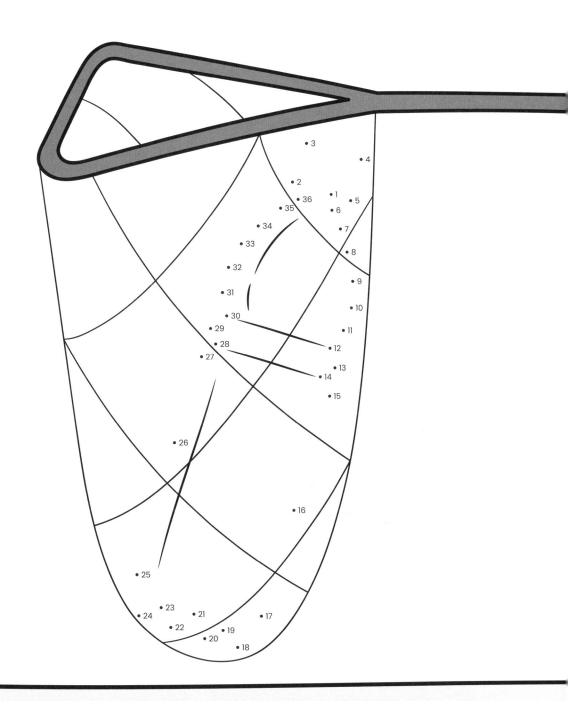

Flag

☐ Found it!

A flag might be a symbol of a country or state, or it might be used as a sign – on a beach, they can tell people whether it's safe to swim.

THAT'S AMAZING!

———

All national flags are rectangular or square in shape, except for one: the flag of Nepal is the shape of two triangles, one on top of the other.

Spot the difference

Circle the odd one out.

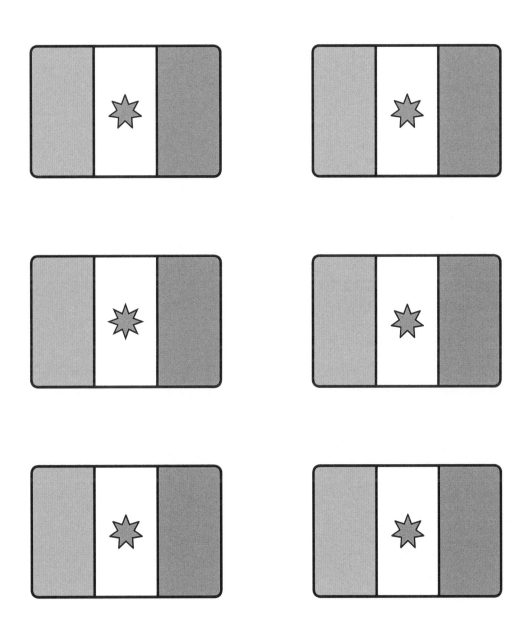

Lifeguard

☑ Found it!

Lifeguards look out for anyone in trouble at the seaside or in a swimming pool. They have special training so that they can teach people how to be safe by the water, prevent accidents, give first aid and help in an emergency.

THAT'S AMAZING!

Lifeguards often sit on a high chair so that they can see as far as possible. Being high up also means that it's easy for everyone else to see where they are.

Numbers

Help the lifeguard to count how many swimmers there are. If 6 swimmers go home how many are there remaining? Use the number line if you need it.

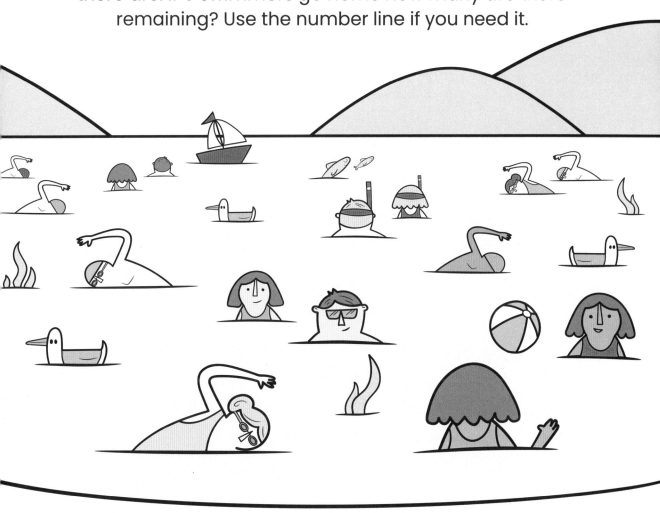

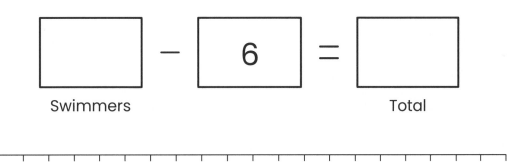

	−	6	=	
Swimmers				Total

0 1 2 3 4 5 6 7 8 9 10 11 12 13 14 15 16 17 18 19 20

Surfboard

☑ Found it!

Surfers use a board to ride the surface of moving waves. It's hard to learn how to do it, but great fun.

THAT'S AMAZING!

The biggest wave ever surfed measured 24.4 m (80 ft) tall! The record was set in 2017 by surfer Rodrigo Koxa.

Telling the time

The surfer needs to leave the beach at 4 o'clock each day. How long does she have left?

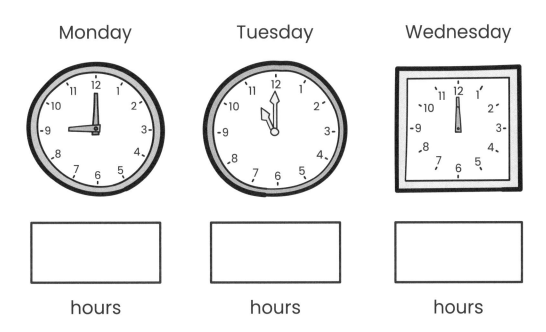

Monday

hours

Tuesday

hours

Wednesday

hours

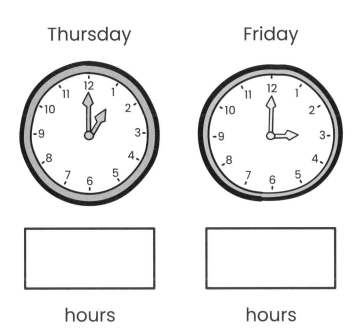

Thursday

hours

Friday

hours

Paddle board

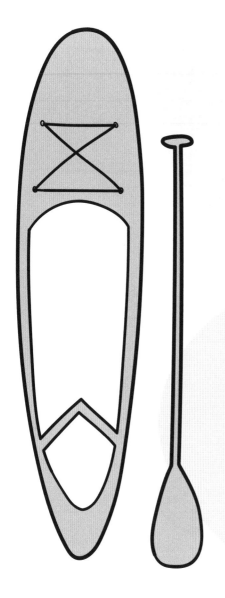

☐ Found it!

Paddleboards are like big surfboards. You can stand up or kneel down to paddle them. It's easier to kneel down if you're a beginner.

THAT'S AMAZING!

Some boats are paddled standing up. In the city of Venice in Italy, flat-bottomed boats called gondolas are rowed by a 'gondolier' using a single oar at the back of the boat.

Wordsearch

Look for the 10 words hidden in the wordsearch puzzle. The hidden words will run down and across. There are no words that run backwards or on a diagonal.

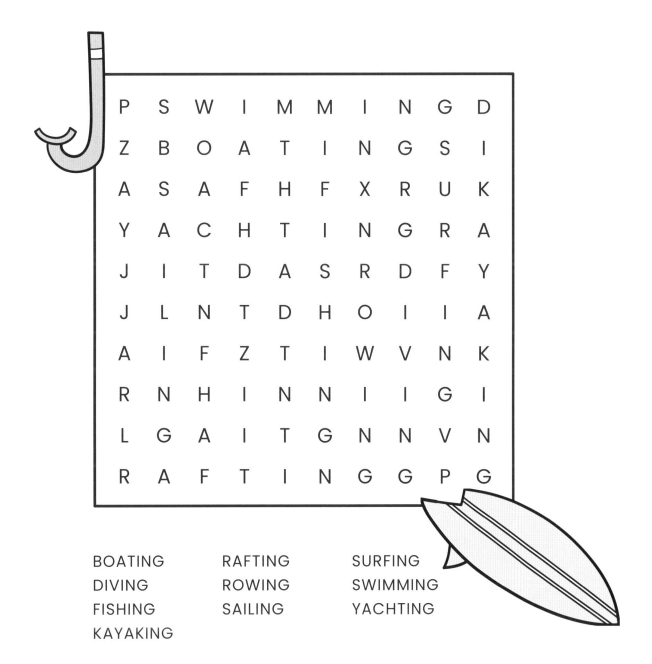

```
P  S  W  I  M  M  I  N  G  D
Z  B  O  A  T  I  N  G  S  I
A  S  A  F  H  F  X  R  U  K
Y  A  C  H  T  I  N  G  R  A
J  I  T  D  A  S  R  D  F  Y
J  L  N  T  D  H  O  I  I  A
A  I  F  Z  T  I  W  V  N  K
R  N  H  I  N  N  I  I  G  I
L  G  A  I  T  G  N  N  V  N
R  A  F  T  I  N  G  G  P  G
```

BOATING   RAFTING   SURFING
DIVING   ROWING   SWIMMING
FISHING   SAILING   YACHTING
KAYAKING

Canoe or kayak

☐ Found it!

A kayak is different from a
canoe – in a canoe you have to
kneel, but you sit in a kayak, and
canoes use paddles with one
blade instead of two in a kayak.
Both are fun to paddle!

THAT'S AMAZING!

The oldest boat that
still exists is a canoe
that dates from around
10,000 years ago.

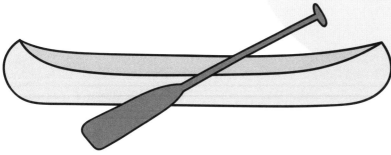

Maze

Help the canoe to find the river that leads to the ocean.

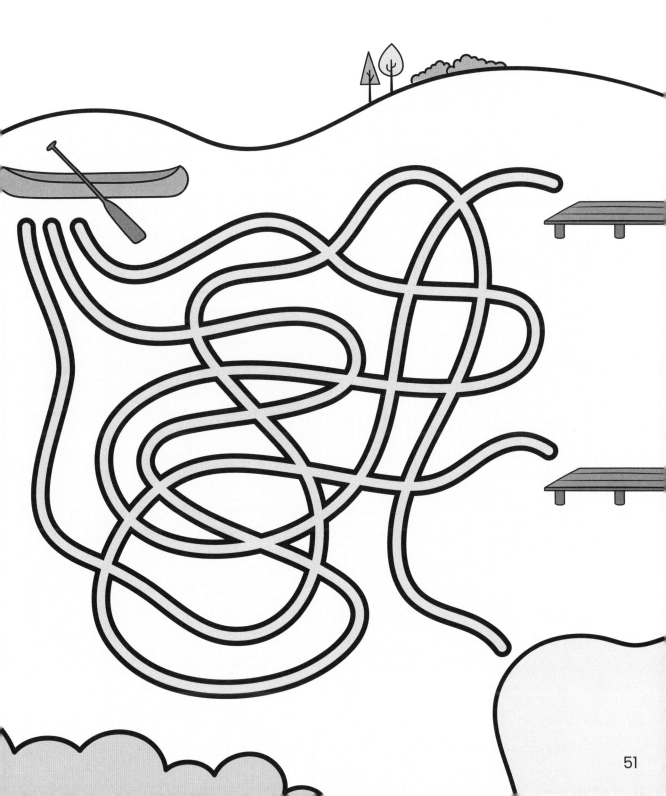

Ship

☐ Found it!

A ship is a large boat. Boats are used to transport people and objects or just for fun. They might be powered by people, like rowing boats and kayaks, by the wind or a motor.

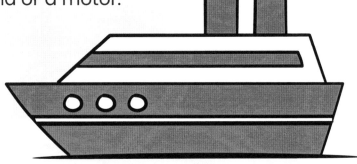

THAT'S AMAZING!

People have been using boats to get around since prehistoric times. The first people to arrive in Australia 40,000 years ago, had to cross 90 km (over 55 mi) of open sea – we don't know what their boats or rafts looked like.

Spot the difference

Can you spot 5 differences between the pictures?

Buoy

☑ Found it!

A buoy is a floating marker in the sea. Buoys might mark a safe channel for ships, or an area where it's safe to swim.

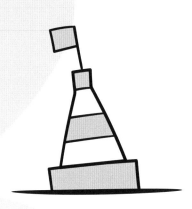

THAT'S AMAZING!

Weather buoys are used at sea to collect information about temperature, wind and ocean currents.

Matching pairs

Can you draw a line to link the number 1 boat with the number 1 buoy and so on, without crossing the lines or hitting the other boats or buoys?

Solutions

Page 07

F I S H

C R A B

S H R I M P

S Q U I D

M U S S E L

S C A L L O P

Page 09

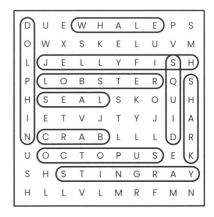

CRAB   OCTOPUS   SQUID
DOLPHIN   SEAL   STINGRAY
JELLYFISH   SHARK   WHALE
LOBSTER

Page 11

Page 13

8 + 10 = 18

Beach   Total

0 1 2 3 4 5 6 7 8 9 10 11 12 13 14 15 16 17 18 19 20

Solutions

Page 15

Page 21

Page 23

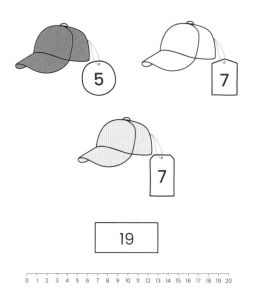

19

0 1 2 3 4 5 6 7 8 9 10 11 12 13 14 15 16 17 18 19 20

Page 25

45
minutes

15
minutes

30
minutes

Solutions

Page 27

Page 29

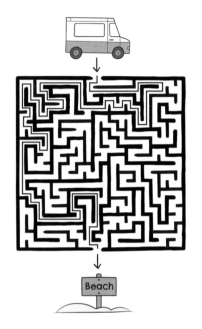

Page 31

Page 33

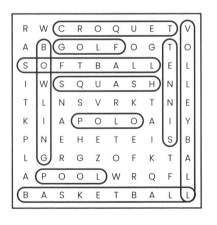

BASKETBALL   POLO   SQUASH
BOWLING   POOL   TENNIS
CROQUET   SOFTBALL   VOLLEYBALL
GOLF

Solutions

Page 37

M U D

S A N D

R O C K S

S H E L L S

W A T E R

F O S S I L S

Page 39

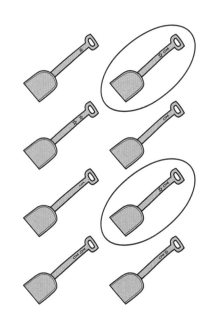

Page 41

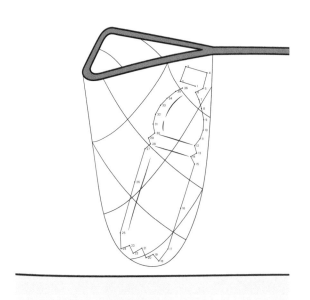

Page 43

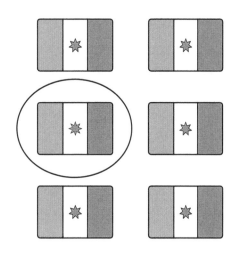

Solutions

Page 45

15	−	6	=	9
Swimmers				Total

0 1 2 3 4 5 6 7 8 9 10 11 12 13 14 15 16 17 18 19 20

Page 47

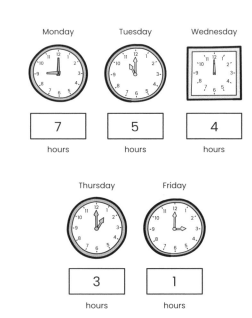

Monday	Tuesday	Wednesday
7	5	4
hours	hours	hours

Thursday	Friday
3	1
hours	hours

Page 49

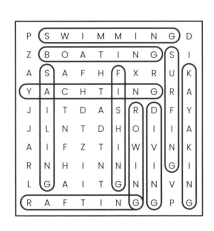

BOATING   RAFTING   SURFING
DIVING   ROWING   SWIMMING
FISHING   SAILING   YACHTING
KAYAKING

Page 51

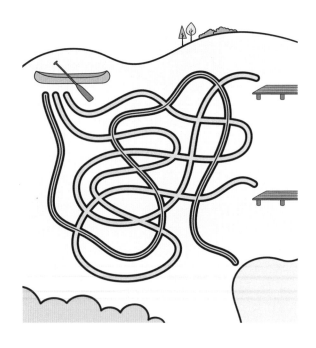

Solutions

Page 53

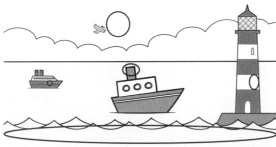

Page 55

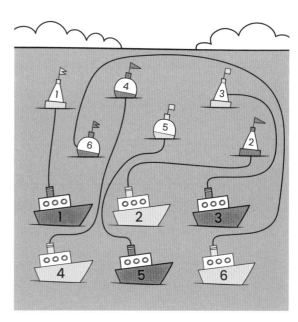

Notes on my finds

_____

_____

_____

_____

_____

_____

_____

_____

_____

_____

_____

_____

_____

Chart of my finds

Finds by:

....

Use this chart as an index to quickly locate your finds within the book, or you can cut it out of the book and use it to find things on your travels. An adult can also use this page to confirm your finds!

Ball	☐	p.32
Bucket	☐	p.36
Buoy	☐	p.54
Canoe/kayak	☐	p.50
Crab	☐	p.10
Drink	☐	p.30
Fish	☐	p.08
Flag	☐	p.42
Flying disk	☐	p.34
Hat	☐	p.22
Ice cream	☐	p.28
Lifeguard	☐	p.44
Net	☐	p.40

Paddle board	☐	p.48
Rock pool	☐	p.16
Sandcastle	☐	p.18
Seagull	☐	p.06
Seaweed	☐	p.14
Shell	☐	p.12
Ship	☐	p.52
Spade	☐	p.38
Sunscreen	☐	p.24
Sunshade	☐	p.20
Surfboard	☐	p.46
Towel	☐	p.26

Find it!

Certificate

This certificate is awarded to:

....

For completing:

Find it! At the beach

....

Date: ....